For Eliot, Cecily and Robin. Stay curious
and keep looking around in wonder. — C.W.

For Jim and Stan — G.H.

MAGIC CAT PUBLISHING

Nature in a Nutshell © 2023 Lucky Cat Publishing Ltd
Text © 2023 Carl Wilkinson
Illustrations © 2023 Grace Helmer

First Published in 2023 by Magic Cat Publishing, an imprint of Lucky Cat Publishing Ltd,
Unit 2 Empress Works, 24 Grove Passage, London E2 9FQ, UK

A catalogue record for this book is available from the British Library.

ISBN 978-1-915569-00-4

The illustrations were created in oil paints
Set in Organika, Above the Sky and Blunt

Published by Rachel Williams and Jenny Broom
Designed by Nicola Price
Edited by Helen Brown
Consultancy by James Doyle

Manufactured in China

9 8 7 6 5 4 3 2 1

MIX
Paper from
responsible sources
FSC® C104723
www.fsc.org

Nature
in a
Nutshell

For Meg, Birdie and Ozzy.

Love from Grace and
Stanley β

Written by
Carl Wilkinson

Illustrated by
Grace Helmer
gracehelmer

MAGIC CAT PUBLISHING

Contents

The Wonders of the Natural World

All around us, the world is working wonders. From the birth of a star to the formation of a fossil, some of the most spectacular moments in nature are out of our reach, and can be easy to miss.

This book unfolds these natural wonders into perfectly formed stories, told frame by frame. Some of them happen slowly, over days, weeks or years – like a stalactite growing to meet a stalagmite, or an acorn becoming an oak tree – while other things happen every day, like an apple falling from a tree, or day turning to night.

Enjoy each story, then step outside and explore the wonders of the natural world for yourself.

A Tiny Acorn
Becomes a Mighty Oak Tree

There's something magical about an ancient oak tree.

It's home to many forms of life, from the squirrels and beetles that scurry around its roots to the jays that bury its fallen acorns.

And every mighty oak tree starts life as a tiny acorn. . .

It's a bright, autumnal day, and this clever jay is collecting fallen acorns from around the base of an old oak.

He will bury them today and return to find them when the cold winter comes. . . if he can remember where he put them!

Look! This tiny acorn hasn't been collected by the jay. It's survived the winter as it's been protected by a thicket of brambles.

When spring comes, the soil begins to warm. The tiny acorn starts to grow. . .

swelling. . . splitting. . . sending down a tap root.

A pale green shoot pushes off the acorn's outer casing and reaches for light.

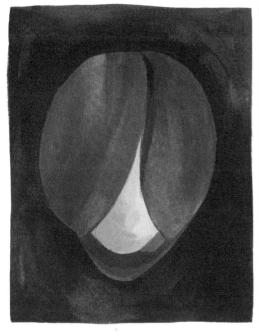

Eight months after the acorn fell, the sapling's first leaves unfurl, searching for the warm sun.

From 10,000 acorns, only one will grow up to be an oak tree.

Meanwhile, tiny roots begin to drink the water-rich soil, drawing up minerals to feed the hungry young tree.

Some types of wasp can cause oak trees to produce large, round growths called galls. In the past, these were used to make ink. Some of the most important texts from history - including Newton's theories and Mozart's music - were written using ink from oak trees.

And now we wait. It will be almost 50 years before the tree produces acorns of its own.

Whale Song
Echoes Through the Ocean

The haunting song of the humpback whale is a magical sound that belongs to the underwater world.

Using groans, deep rumbling noises and high-pitched whines, this gentle giant communicates across vast oceans. But what is it saying and how does it sing?

In the wide, open ocean, a whale surfaces to take a lungful of air. . .

before sinking beneath the water's surface again.

Like a human, a humpback whale has vocal chords that vibrate when air is forced over them. Whale's voice box is more complex than ours, though. It is made up of folds connected to air sacs in the throat, which scientists believe allow Whale to move air over the folds to make sounds without having to breathe out as we do.

Whale spots an attractive female, and, to impress her – and ward off competitors – he begins his song, making whoops, barks and groans which he performs in a sequence called a 'phrase'.

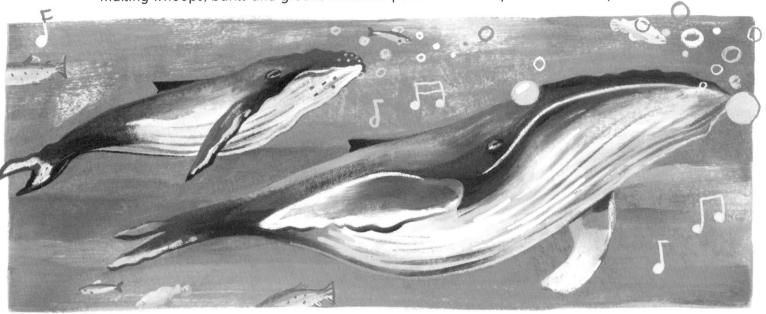

A series of phrases are put together to make a 'theme'. Whale then combines these into a song, which can last up to 15 minutes.

Having done his best to impress, Whale returns to the surface to blow out air through the twin blow holes on his head, before taking another lungful and diving beneath the waves to start his song. . .

all over again.

A Desert Meadow
Bursts into Bloom

A dry and dusty desert comes alive, filled with vibrant wildflowers.

Very little can survive the hot valley floor but, once in a while, it explodes with life and colour.

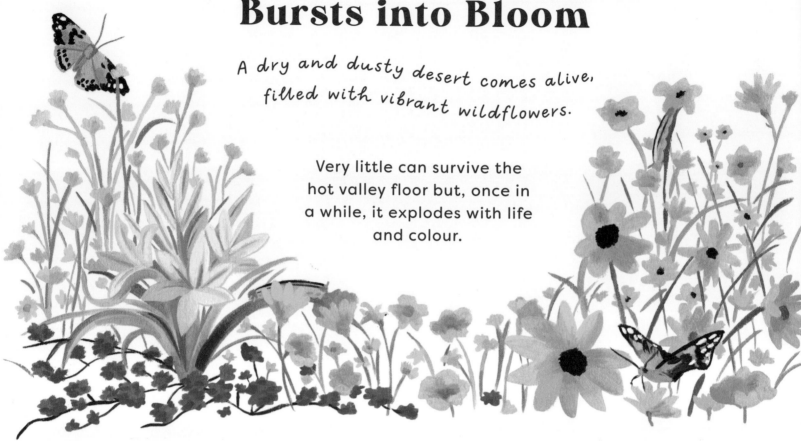

Given the right conditions, seeds can lie dormant in soil for many years. Scientists have managed to successfully 'germinate', or grow, seeds dating from as far back as 30,000 years ago.

Just below the desert floor lie thousands of wildflower seeds, waiting patiently through the months of drought.

Until a drop of rain falls. . .
then another. . .

The sky opens and heavy rain
soaks the parched earth.

The warmth from the rain begins
to wake the seeds.

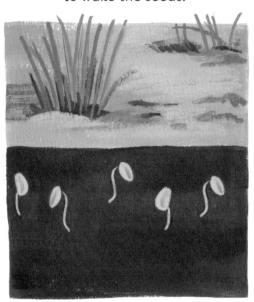

The seeds sprout and grow, bursting through the floor. . .

growing up and up, in perfect harmony.

Wildflowers carpet the landscape in
a vivid rainbow of colours, welcoming
wildlife from across the valley.

What a spectacular
superbloom!

A Stalactite Grows
to Meet a Stalagmite

Drip! Drip! Hidden underground, rock spikes dangle from the ceiling while stone rises up to meet them, lit by a thousand twinkling glow-worms.

These dangling spikes are called stalactites and they form when mineral-saturated water drips from a cave roof. The growing spires beneath them are called stalagmites.

Will they meet? Let's wait and see. . .

Water trickles through cracks in limestone rock, collecting minerals along the way and carrying them deeper underground.

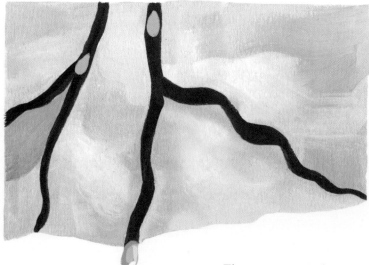

The water reaches the roof of a cave and begins to slowly drip on to the floor below.

Each falling water droplet leaves behind a tiny trace on the ceiling. . .

which can grow into a delicate, hollow straw. . .

before filling out to become the cone of a stalactite!

Stalactites and stalagmites grow very, very slowly. The fastest increase in length by about 3 millimetres a year, but most don't grow that quickly and can take tens of thousands of years to develop.

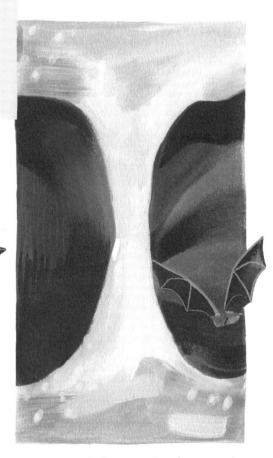

Meanwhile, the minerals are also deposited on the floor of the cave.

These slowly form a mound that looks like the stump of a melted candle. . . a stalagmite!

Over tens of thousands of years, the stalactite and stalagmite will grow until they meet, forming a pillar.

An Apple Falls from a Tree

What goes up must come down...

Throughout the universe there is an invisible force called gravity that pulls objects towards each other.

Isaac Newton was a scientist who worked out the rules of gravity. Isaac saw an apple fall to the ground and wondered why the apple fell straight down, rather than sideways or even upward.

He discovered the force of gravity depends on how much mass an object has, and that the pull of gravity between objects gets smaller the further apart they are. Let's see his theory in action...

Gravity is what keeps our feet on the ground! It is the force that holds the Moon in orbit around the Earth and the Earth in orbit around the Sun.

The weather is cool and wet, and the orchard's apple tree is ready to shed its fruit.

Snap! The apple breaks away from the branch.

It falls. . . down. . . down. . . down. . .

Bump! The apple thumps on to the grass beneath the tree.

It bounces up. . . up. . . up. . .

It bounces once more. . .

Both the apple and the Earth are objects with gravity, but the Earth is much, much bigger, and so its pull on the apple is much stronger than the apple's pull on the Earth. And so the apple falls to the Earth and not the other way around.

Bump! The apple thumps on to the grass again.

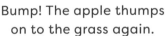

Until finally coming to a halt. The worms rejoice – this is gravity at work!

The Northern Lights
Flicker Across the Sky

A magical light show sweeps across the horizon, bathing frozen lakes and snow-covered trees in a mysterious glow.

In mythology, the lights were thought to be a bridge built by the gods to link the land and sky. Today, we know they're caused by particles from the Sun hitting Earth's magnetic field, which makes atoms in the Earth's atmosphere glow. . .

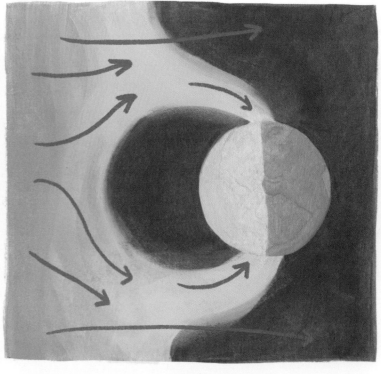

There's an explosion on the surface of the Sun - one of hundreds happening every day! Charged particles are blown into space, hurtling towards Earth. . .

Earth's magnetic field acts as a protective bubble. On the sunny side of the Earth, the particles bounce off and rush towards the North and South Poles. . .

More particles whizz past Earth before being dragged back to the poles on the night side.

The particles rain down on Earth, following the invisible lines of the magnetic field in a ring around the Arctic and Antarctic Circles.

The variations in colour are due to the type of gas particles that are colliding. Pale green and pink are the most common, but shades of red, yellow, blue and purple have been seen.

The lights flicker and dance as the solar storm brings waves of particles that dash to Earth. They collide with atoms of oxygen and nitrogen in the atmosphere, which become excited and start to glow!

This magical light show can last for hours, or just a few minutes. What an amazing sight to see!

A Fairy Ring
Grows in a Meadow

A delicate circle of mushrooms has formed where fairies and elves once danced. . .

Fairy rings are arcs or circles of mushrooms that can appear naturally. They are also known as 'elf circles' or 'pixie rings'. Once upon a time, people believed that they were created by the dancing feet of fairies and elves – or even by fiery dragons or witches!

Today, we know that they are caused by a fungus growing underground. It spreads outwards through the grass roots, producing circles of tiny mushrooms. . .

When a mushroom matures, it starts to shed 'spores', or seeds, which are carried on the breeze to other parts of the forest.

The spores find their way into the soil and tiny roots called 'mycelium' begin to spread outwards.

As the mycelium spreads, it attaches itself to the grass roots to absorb nutrients.

The mycelium repels water and so the grass it has attached to dries out and begins to turn brown. . .

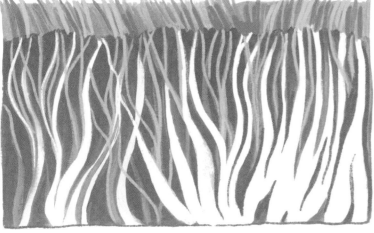 

while the turf directly outside the affected area is slightly lusher and greener than normal.

The circular front of the mycelium slowly grows outwards and forms an expanding ring of dry, brown grass.

During summer and early autumn, the mycelium fruits and forms a magical ring of small mushrooms that sprout above ground, just like the footprints of fairies. . .

The oldest fairy ring is in France and is thought to date back 700 years!

The Sea
Creates a Sculpture Park

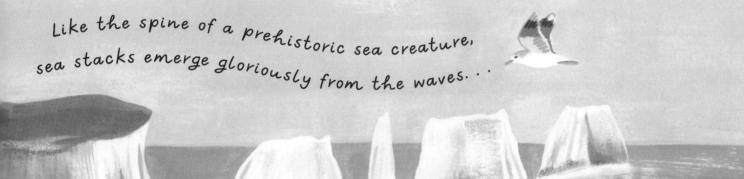

Like the spine of a prehistoric sea creature, sea stacks emerge gloriously from the waves. . .

Crafted by nature, sea stacks slowly take shape when softer rock from the coastline is eroded by the sea. But how do they form? And why do they look like they do?

Millions of years ago, a spine of hard chalk sat at the centre of this island. When the earth's plates moved, the chalk twisted and folded.

As waves crashed up against it, cracks formed in the cliff, where softer rock was eroded by the crashing waves.

Waves continued to wear away the rock, creating an arch. . .

The headland (the steep-sided point of land that projects from a coastline) narrowed, worn away on both sides to form a long, sharp ridge of rock that reached into the sea.

which over time collapsed to leave behind a towering sea stack, perfect for nesting birds.

Over the next million years, the headland took on great, towering sculptural shapes.

Today, wild storms continue to throw huge waves up the sea stacks, with rocks collapsing into the water below with a colossal splash!

The tallest sea stack in the world is Ball's Pyramid, off the coast of Australia in the Pacific Ocean. It stands at 562 metres high and is all that remains of a vast volcano that once stood there millions of years ago.

A Star is Born

Look up on a clear night and you'll see the sky filled with thousands of twinkling stars.

A star is a large ball of burning gas far out in space.
But how is a star born? And what happens when it stops burning?

Swirling throughout most galaxies, there are huge clouds of gas called 'nebulae', which can be seen without a telescope on a clear night.

Gravity causes the cloud to fall in on itself and become more closely packed.

The temperature rises and the cloud begins to spin into a ball.

The centre of the ball becomes hotter and hotter until a reaction causes a baby star called a 'protostar' to form.

The new star now begins to grow, taking around 50 million years to become a mature star.

How long it will burn for depends on how big it is!

Eventually, after millions more years, the star will come to the end of its life. During this part of its life, some stars glow and fade, glow and fade, which is called 'pulsating'.

Sometimes, the dying star will explode in a giant 'supernova', producing a spectacular light show. At other times, it sends a cloud of gas back into space. . . and a star is ready to be born all over again.

Our Sun, which is also a star, has an estimated lifespan of about 10 billion years and was formed about 4.6 billion years ago.

A Tree Brings Fresh Air to the Forest

Take a slow, deep breath in...
You've just filled your
lungs with oxygen.

Now, let your breath out. There goes carbon dioxide. But where did the oxygen come from and where did that carbon dioxide go?

Throughout the day, trees and plants turn the carbon dioxide we breathe out into food to help them grow, and oxygen for us to breathe. This process is called 'photosynthesis'.

Without photosynthesis there would be no life on Earth. Trees and plants act like your lungs; they make the air breathable.

It's a sunny morning as the light from the sun catches the dew on the leaves of a giant kapok tree.

Far below the canopy, the tree's roots are sucking up water from deep in the ground. The roots take the water on a journey through the trunk's tubes to all its branches and leaves.

Little holes on the bottom of the tree's leaves start to let in carbon dioxide from the air.

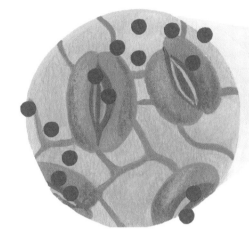

Inside the leaf, there is a substance called 'chlorophyll'. This green pigment gives leaves their green colour.

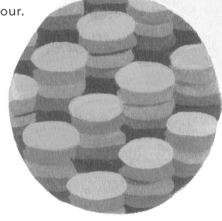

At the end of the day, when the sun goes down, the leaf stops turning carbon dioxide into oxygen. . .

Planting more trees is an important part of helping to protect and improve our world.

Like a mini solar panel, when light from the sun hits the leaf, the chlorophyll turns the carbon dioxide from the air and the water from the ground into a kind of sugar called 'glucose'.

This is food for the leaf. It also produces oxygen, which the tree releases back into the air.

Until the sun rises, and the cycle begins again.

Sand Dunes
Migrate Across the Sahara

The wind whispers over the gentle curves of the dunes, whipping up sand as a camel train navigates the horizon.

Millions of years ago, the Sahara desert was covered with water — the ancient sea of Tethys. When the sea dried up, the land turned to desert and formed into a gently undulating landscape of dunes, which look like the waves of an inland sea, frozen in time. But look closer: the sand is shifting and the restless dunes are always on the move. . .

As wind pushes grains of sand against small objects, such as bushes or rocks, mounds begin to form.

The mounds grow taller and taller.

The side sheltered from the wind becomes steeper and steeper.

Sand dunes have been known to sing. Thanks to the billions of grains of shifting sand rubbing against each other, dunes can produce booming or humming sounds that are amplified by their shape. Some have measured as loud as a motorbike!

This sheltered side eventually collapses, sending an avalanche of sand cascading down into the valley.

Meanwhile, sand continues to rise on the windy side, adding to the grains that have recently slipped.

The dune creeps across the desert like a rolling wave, moving in slow motion. . .

A Gust of Wind
Sends a Kite Soaring

A kite loops and twirls, dancing in the breeze...

Wind is the movement of air caused by differences in temperature. When the Sun warms the surface of the Earth, it also warms the air, which then rises.

As this warm air rises, cooler air rushes in to replace it, and you have wind! The power of this moving air can send a kite racing across the sky...

It's a windy afternoon in the park... the perfect day for flying a kite!

The secret to kite flying is catching the wind. . . at just the right moment.

Holding it high, the kite trembles as it catches the breeze.

People have been flying kites for thousands of years. Some of the first kites in China were made of bamboo canes and silk.

The wind fills the kite. . .

and the string goes taut.

Off it flies, into the sky. Up, up and away!

As the wind pushes against the kite, it generates lift and races into the sky. Higher and higher it goes, as more string is let out so that it can climb.

The kite soars upwards to join the others, bobbing, swaying, looping in the breeze.

25

The North Star
Points the Way

Twinkling stars sweep out in a big circle as they move through the night sky.

When darkness falls, the stars appear to move across the night sky as Earth spins on itself, making a complete turn every 24 hours.

But there is one star in the night sky that does not appear to move. It is called 'Polaris', or the North Star. Look up on a clear night and let it point the way. . .

The sun starts disappearing below the horizon. . .

and one by one, stars come out to illuminate the night sky.

As Earth spins on its axis, stars appear to slowly move around and around. . . and around.

Gaze up at the night sky for long enough and you'll see these points of starlight turn like a wheel.

At the centre of the wheel sits a single, bright star: Polaris.
Polaris holds still while the entire northern sky appears to move around it.

If you stand facing Polaris, then you're facing the direction north. If you stand with your back to Polaris, you're facing south. You can find it easily, and once you do, you'll see it shining every night.

Polaris is close to 430 light years from Earth and is the brightest star in the constellation.

An Avalanche
Roars Down a Mountainside

A silent stillness hangs in the cold mountain air, until it is broken by a rumbling sound...

An avalanche!

This spectacle occurs when a slab of snow and ice breaks loose and hurtles down a mountainside, carrying rocks and trees with it.

High on the mountainside, three skiers stop to take in the view and savour the silence...

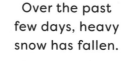

Over the past few days, heavy snow has fallen.

Until it is broken by a strange noise from across the valley.

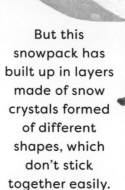

But this snowpack has built up in layers made of snow crystals formed of different shapes, which don't stick together easily.

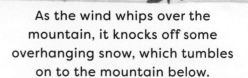

As the wind whips over the mountain, it knocks off some overhanging snow, which tumbles on to the mountain below.

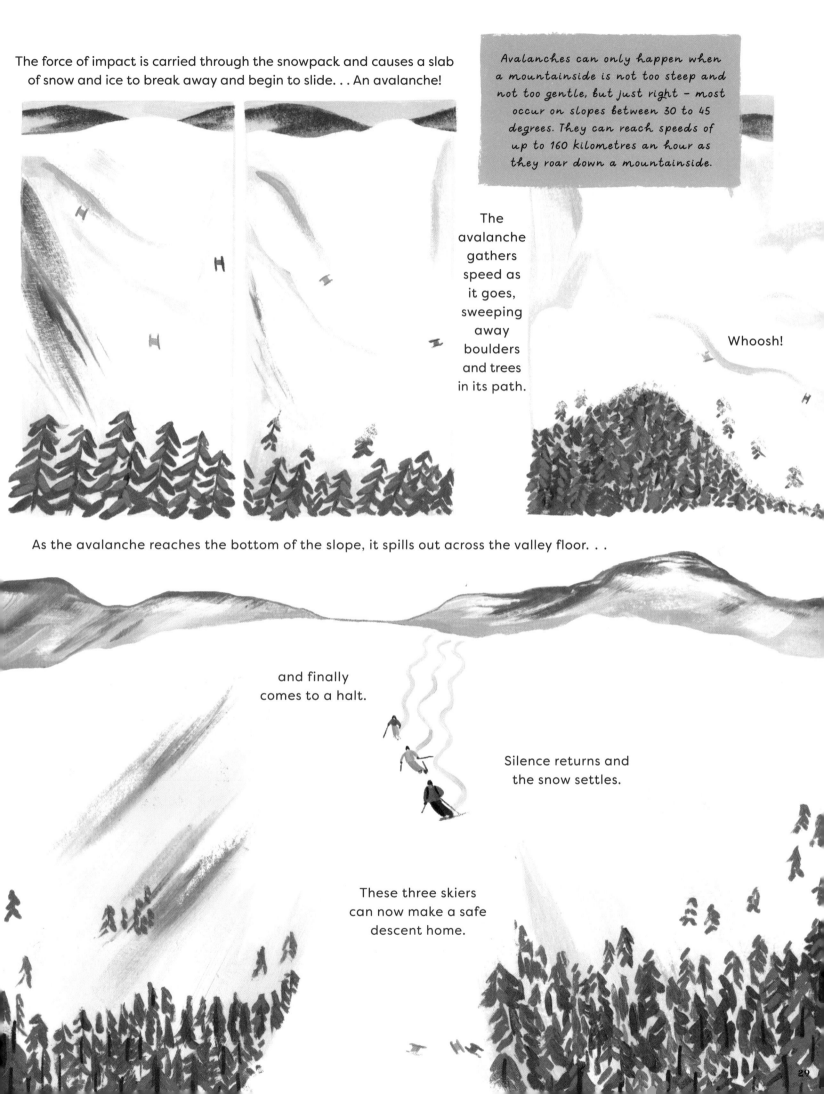

The force of impact is carried through the snowpack and causes a slab of snow and ice to break away and begin to slide. . . An avalanche!

Avalanches can only happen when a mountainside is not too steep and not too gentle, but just right – most occur on slopes between 30 to 45 degrees. They can reach speeds of up to 160 kilometres an hour as they roar down a mountainside.

The avalanche gathers speed as it goes, sweeping away boulders and trees in its path.

Whoosh!

As the avalanche reaches the bottom of the slope, it spills out across the valley floor. . .

and finally comes to a halt.

Silence returns and the snow settles.

These three skiers can now make a safe descent home.

A Dinosaur Fossil Forms

Millions of years ago, dinosaurs walked the Earth.

Fossils are the remains of plants and animals – like dinosaurs – that have been preserved in the earth's natural materials.

All sorts of things can be fossilized: bones, teeth, footprints and, sometimes, an entire skeleton! Let's watch one form over millions of years. . .

When a dinosaur died, the soft, fleshy parts of its body rotted away – or were eaten – leaving only the skeleton.

To have a chance of becoming a fossil, the dinosaur's bones needed to be quickly covered with mud, silt, sand or sediment. This usually happened underwater.

Over millions of years, layers of mud, sand, silt and volcanic ash built up, covering the dinosaur's remains.

Under great pressure from the layers above, these sediments turned to solid rock.

Meanwhile, water seeped into the tiny holes in the dinosaur's bones. The minerals in the water were left behind in the spaces where the bones once were, and slowly turned to stone. . .

As continents moved, volcanoes erupted, mountain ranges grew and sea levels rose and fell, the earth changed, lifting up some of the rocks that contain fossils once buried deep below the ground.

Slowly, wind, rain, ice and the sea eroded the rock around the fossils. . . exposing them, ready for us to discover.

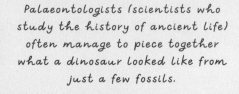

Palaeontologists (scientists who study the history of ancient life) often manage to piece together what a dinosaur looked like from just a few fossils.

An Iceberg Breaks Away

With a groan and a monumental crash, an iceberg as tall as a tower block tumbles into the ocean.

Icebergs are a natural sight in the sea around the North and South Poles, but as the climate changes, warmer air and water are speeding up the melting of glaciers and causing them to break into large icebergs.

A 2-kilometre-thick glacier slowly flows across Antarctica.
When it reaches the Southern Ocean, it creates an ice shelf – a floating tongue of ice.

The seawater begins to melt the underside of the ice shelf until it becomes thinner and weaker, and cracks start to appear.

Finally, part of the ice shelf breaks off, toppling over into the sea with an enormous CRASH!
The birth of an iceberg is known as 'calving'.

The iceberg slowly floats away, carried by the current, and continues to
melt, breaking into smaller pieces as it reaches warmer waters. . .

Antarctica's glaciers are so large
that if they all melted, the world's
sea level would rise by about
60 metres. Most concerningly,
this would mean that countries
like Bangladesh and cities such
as London, New York and Shanghai
would be underwater.

Earthworms Surface
After Rainfall

Following a heavy downpour, the grass is alive with slithering earthworms...

Earthworms live underground and help to keep the soil healthy. But after rainfall, they often come to the surface.

Let's watch as a sudden storm brings an earthworm out of its dark burrow...

Deep underground, this earthworm is eating decaying plant and animal matter, which it breaks down into smaller pieces allowing bacteria and fungi to feed on it and release nutrients.

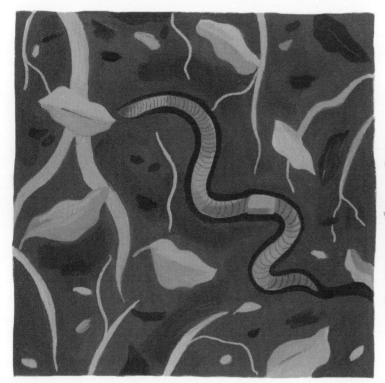

Up above, the sky grows darker and towering rain clouds gather on the horizon.

Gently at first, and then harder, the rain comes down, drumming on the lush, green grass.

The earthworm starts to feel the vibrations of the raindrops and it panics. The raindrops sound like a burrowing predator. . .

To escape the potential danger from below, the earthworm wriggles upwards through the soil.

Could it be a hungry mole?

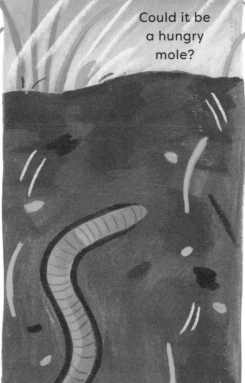

Some birds, such as seagulls, mimic the sound of rain by stamping their feet on the ground to encourage earthworms to the surface to feed on them.

Emerging at the surface, it writhes and squirms to make a quick escape!

Earthworms require moisture to breathe through their skin and find it easier to move across the wet grass than through the dry soil.

The rain stops and the grass is covered with earthworms. But as blackbirds start to circle above, it may not have been such a safe place to escape to!

A Tornado Picks Up Speed
and Races Across the Plains

The hot summer days on the plains can bring about one of nature's most mesmerizing and dangerous displays.

Also known as 'twisters', tornadoes are towering clouds that reach down from the sky to the ground. These powerful, spinning columns of air travel very quickly, destroying everything in their path. . .

It's a hot day, and the heat of the sun warms the ground, causing the air to rise.

Tornadoes form mostly over land and hurricanes form over warm water. Hurricanes are much larger than tornadoes, often building slowly to reach hundreds of kilometres across, but tornadoes can appear suddenly and move very fast.

When this warm, moist air hits the colder, dry air above, it forms huge towering storm clouds called 'cumulonimbus', bringing with it thunder, lightning and rain.

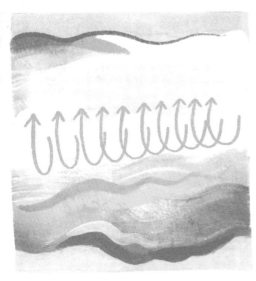

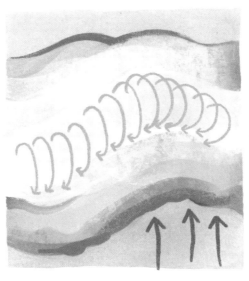

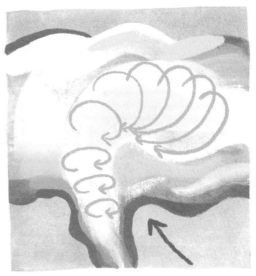

The rising warm air moves very quickly. . .

making the cloud rotate. . .

and the spinning cone of air reaches the ground below.

When it touches the ground, it becomes a tornado, or 'twister'.

And it's off! Racing across the plains with incredible speed.

Tornadoes are difficult to predict and can be just a few metres across or hundreds of metres wide. Some appear and disappear in just a few seconds, but others can last up to an hour. . . moving very quickly across great distances, leaving a path of destruction in their wake.

A Volcano Erupts
and Lava Flows

Earth puts on a natural firework display, lighting up the night sky as a volcano erupts.

As the pressure builds beneath the Earth's surface, underground molten rock is forced upwards.

It spews out of a volcano and sends rivers of lava down its slopes. Smoke, dust and ash rise into the sky above.

The Earth's surface is a thin crust floating on a sea of hot molten rock called magma.

Magma rises through a gap in the crust and is trapped in an area called a magma chamber.

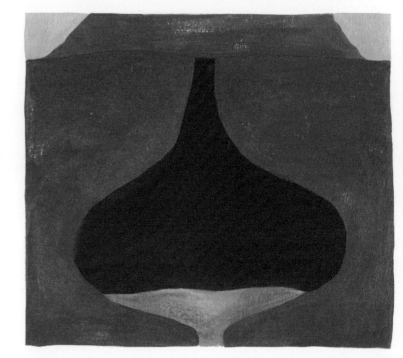

As more magma enters the chamber, pressure builds. . .

The pressure forces the magma through weak points, called vents, in the rock above. . .

Whoosh! It explodes, pushing out the plug of rock blocking its exit, and magma gushes out.

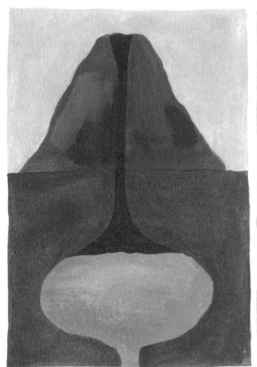

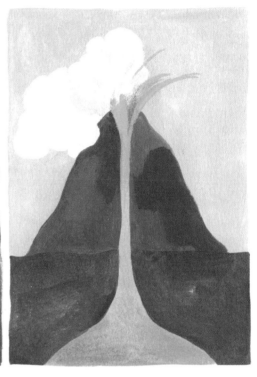

When a volcano erupts underwater, the cooling layers of lava slowly form a cone. After time passes, the cone emerges from the sea to form an island.

Clouds of smoke, dust and ash tower upwards into the sky, stretching for hundreds of kilometres, as the wind carries it.

The magma spills out of the crater and becomes lava, which flows like a river down the sides of the volcano.

Over many months, it cools and hardens to become volcanic rock.

A Tree Springs into Life

Today brings a beautiful blue sky.

The days are getting longer, the birds are starting to sing and deep within the trees something is starting to move...

Spring is here! Trees begin to wake. Watch and listen as we follow a birch tree on its journey through the season...

Spring sunshine wakes the birds sheltering in the birch tree.

Thirsty after a long winter, the tree draws up water and minerals through its roots from deep in the soil.

Then, it releases the food stored in its roots, which flows as a sugary fluid called 'sap'.

Press your ear to the trunk of a birch, beech or cherry tree in early spring and you may hear the sap rising. Listen carefully for a gushing and popping sound. The tree is alive!

The water and sap flow along a network of tiny tubes that run below the surface of the bark all the way to the very tips of each branch.

The sap feeds the fresh young buds. They swell. . . and swell. . . and then burst open!

They reveal bright green leaves held together by a web of veins.

This tree has now been fed and is ready for a new season of growth.

Light Travels
300,000 Kilometres in a Second

Light is a type of energy that that makes it possible for us to see the beautiful world around us.

From the first rays of light at sunrise to the final glow on the horizon at sunset, our days are lit by our very own star, the Sun. Let's lie back on a sunny day and imagine the journey this sunlight has been on. . .

The Sun never stops shining. All that light is actually energy released by the Sun in all directions.

The nearest star to our Sun is 4.24 light years away. It takes that long for the light we see from that star to reach us. So, when you look up on a beautiful, clear night it is like looking back in time.

The Sun's energy is released in little particles called 'photons'. They vibrate like ripples on the ocean's water while whizzing in straight lines out into space.

To get to us on Earth, the light travels at a top speed of close to 300,000 kilometres per second.

That's so fast that it could go around the world 7.5 times in a single second. This is known as the speed of light and is a kind of speed limit for the universe - nothing can travel faster than light.

The Earth is almost 150 million kilometres away from the Sun. . .

so the warm sunshine on the beach took around eight minutes to travel there. But it's worth the wait – bliss!

Day Turns to Night
as Our World Revolves

Day follows night and night follows day as our world performs a graceful rotation.

The Sun rises in the morning and sets in the evening – or so it seems. . . In fact, it's us that moves. As the Earth travels around the Sun, it turns on its axis. When the side of the Earth you are on faces the Sun, it's daytime. When you're facing away, it's night-time.

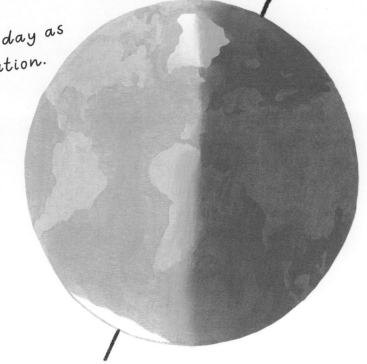

Because Earth is always turning, it seems as if the Sun is rising in the east and setting in the west. This is one of the reasons Earth is so friendly to life, allowing parts to stay at a comfortable temperature, as they are bathed in light during the day and in darkness at night. . .

It's early in the morning and the sky begins to lighten – first blue, then pink – as the Sun peeks above the horizon in the east, its low rays casting long shadows over the city.

As the Earth slowly turns, the Sun climbs in the sky. . . higher. . . and higher. . . and higher. . .

By the middle of the day, the Sun shines directly overhead, bathing these city dwellers in light and heat.

As the Earth continues to turn, the Sun sinks in the sky. . . lower. . . and lower. . . and lower. . .

When the end of the day draws near, the Sun disappears below the horizon in the west and the temperature drops.

The sky begins to darken over the city as it faces away from the Sun and night falls.

The Earth turns on its axis once every 24 hours. So even if you're standing still at the equator, you're whizzing round at about 1,600 kilometres an hour!

As a hungry fox has her feast late at night, Earth continues to spin, gearing up to bring the Sun out again tomorrow.

The Ocean Puts on a Light Show

Star-like shapes of luminous green, a spectacular blue shimmering glow. . . the ocean is a natural wonder.

In the ocean's dark waters live many creatures that have the unearthly ability to glow, emitting a strange light from their cells in a spectacular process known as 'bioluminescence'.

As the stars twinkle above and the waves break on the sandy shore, millions of tiny bioluminescent plankton float in its waters. And with every splash, every jump, every movement, the ocean sparkles. . .

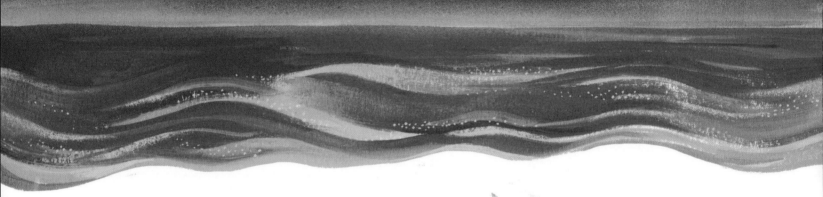

Standing at the water's edge, this swimmer steps forward. . .

and dives beneath the surface of the lagoon.

Small organisms called plankton are gently drifting with the ocean currents. . .

But with each swimmer's stroke, they start to react!

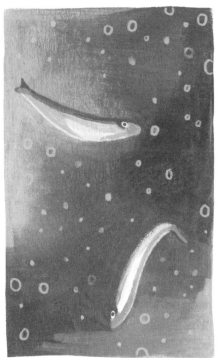

The movement causes the plankton to mix together two chemicals in their tiny bodies to produce a warning flash of blue-green light. . .

One of the best places to see bioluminescent plankton is in the warm sea and lagoons around Puerto Rico in Central America.

The light show continues all through the night as the stars above are outnumbered by the star-like shapes sparkling beneath the water.

A Geyser Shoots Water into the Sky

There's a rumbling beneath your feet...
Old Faithful is about to blow!

A spectacular jet of water suddenly shoots into the sky, erupting in a cloud of steam.

Geysers are rare displays, caused when water deep underground is heated by hot molten rock, or magma.

As the water warms, it rises through the rock before it comes to the boil, sending a towering column of steam into the air. Look out, here comes another eruption!

Drip... drip... drip...

As rainwater trickles through the rock, it finds its way into an underground reservoir above a large pool of magma.

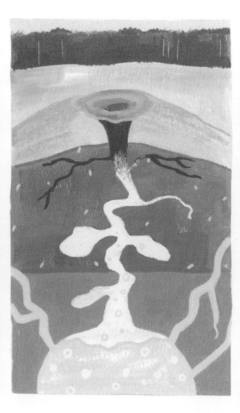

The magma heats the water, and it starts to rise up through cracks in the rock.

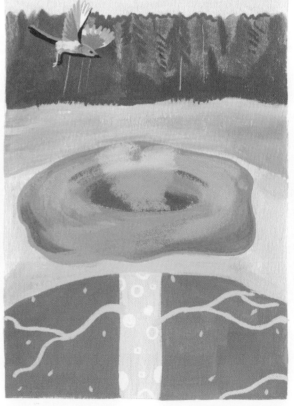

It boils and turns the water into steam. The steam takes up more space than water...

But, near the surface, a restriction in the rock slows the steam's escape and the pressure builds. . .

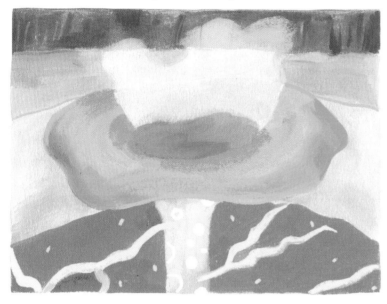

and builds. . . until boiling water shoots from the ground!

First in a small spurt. . . then taller. . .

and taller. . . until a towering plume of steam and water rises 40 metres high into the clear blue sky!

When the underground reservoir is empty, the geyser stops.

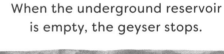

There are only around 1,000 geysers in the whole world and more than half of them are in Yellowstone National Park in the USA.

The water trickles back down to refill the reservoir ready for the next spectacular show.

A Log Burns Brightly

The bright flames flicker and dance in the darkness...

Sitting around a campfire, you can feel its warmth, smell the smoke and hear it crackle and spit.

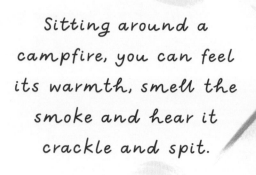

For thousands of years, we have used fire for heat, light and to cook our food. When wood is added to a fire, flames leap higher as it begins to blaze.

But what is a fire and how does wood combust to produce heat and light?

For a fire to burn, it needs three things: fuel, oxygen and heat. If you remove any one of these, the fire will go out.

With the sky growing dark, these campmates put a dry log on the campfire.

The log heats up and the outer edges start to catch fire, crackling and burning brightly.

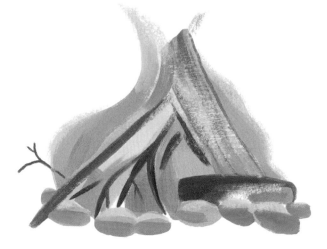

The heat excites the atoms in the wood and, as they get hotter, they start to break apart and are released as gases.

A chemical reaction begins as these gases combine with the oxygen in the air around the fire. This reaction produces heat, which keeps the log hot enough to carry on burning and release more gases in a continuous process.

As the log burns, it releases energy as heat and light - the flames - perfect for toasting marshmallows!

The fire slowly turns the wood to gas, which is released as smoke, and heat energy.

What remains in the campfire is the powdery grey-white ash, and without the light and heat from the fire, it's time for bed for these tired campmates.

Cave Crystals
Grow to Gigantic Sizes

Towering crystals glisten and gleam
in the beam of a miner's lamp...

Deep underground in the Naica
mine in Mexico lie some of the largest
natural crystals ever discovered.

When Mexican miners first explored the
Cave of Crystals, they were amazed to
find 15-metre-long pillars of the mineral
gypsum. How did these crystals reach
such gigantic proportions?

The rising water was rich in minerals and heated to
high temperatures by the lake of magma beneath it.

Millions of years ago, hot molten rock pushed upwards
and forced water into the underground caves
290 metres beneath this Naica mine.

Meanwhile, cooler water from the surface
trickled down to join this rising hot water.
A chemical reaction began. . .

A long period of time passed before the water reached the perfect temperature for crystals to begin to form – just below 58 degrees Celsius.

These crystals grew so slowly that it took an incredible 200 years for a layer of minerals just the thickness of a sheet of paper to build up!

As the water remained at the perfect temperature, more crystals formed and they became enormous. . .

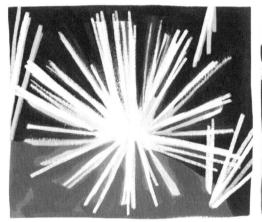

and over 20 years ago were discovered weighing 50 tonnes each!

When Mexican miners entered the Cave of Crystals, the mineral-rich water was pumped out and it was a sweltering 50 degrees Celsius and more than 90 per cent humidity. This made it unbearable for people to spend more than ten minutes at a time inside the cave.

A Waterfall Creates a Secret Grotto

Deep in the jungle, cool water cascades off a rocky ledge and gently falls into a clear plunge pool below.

The water passes into the jungle, nourishing all the animals that live within it.

Waterfalls form as rivers flow from hard rock to soft rock. These beautiful creations are often found tucked away in forests and jungles, and create small picturesque caves called grottos. Let's watch a waterfall sculpt a secret grotto behind its curtain of water...

The river flows across a slab of hard rock before it reaches the edge of the waterfall.

The world's highest uninterrupted waterfall is Angel Falls in Venezuela. It has a height of 979 metres and a plunge of 807 metres!

Water pours over the lip of rock, carrying stones as it takes flight, falling down towards the clear blue plunge pool below.

Water and stones churn, gradually wearing away the softer rock. This is called 'erosion'.

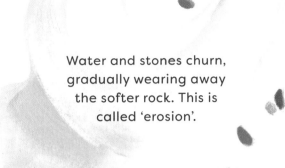

Erosion cuts away at the cliff behind, creating a small opening called a rock shelter, hidden away behind the waterfall – a grotto!

The water continues to fall, churning the plunge pool and wearing away the rock until. . .

the overhanging rock cracks. . . teeters. . . and finally breaks off, tumbling into the plunge pool below!

The process repeats over time, and the waterfall moves upstream to carve out a new grotto, waiting to be explored by those lucky enough to find it.

A Black Hole
Swallows a Star

At the heart of most galaxies lies a dark secret. . . a black hole.

Black holes are one of the biggest mysteries in the universe. They are so dense, with such strong gravitational pull, that they suck in everything around them, including light. . . and even this enormous star. Let's orbit a black hole as it is caught in the act of swallowing a star. . .

This star is being drawn in by the black hole's huge gravitational pull.

The star begins to orbit the black hole, round. . . and round. . . and round like water circling a plughole.

The star is stretched. . . longer. . . and longer. . . and longer. . .

Until it is shredded! It is pulled apart by the black hole and turned into long spaghetti-like streamers of burning gas and dust that disappear from view as they tip over the 'event horizon', a point beyond which nothing can escape and time stands still.

Any objects that fall into black holes are stretched to breaking point. Their gravity doesn't disappear from the universe it is added to the densely packed mass of the black hole.

The star spirals down. . . down. . . down. . . into the black hole in one final brilliant flash of light. Wow!

 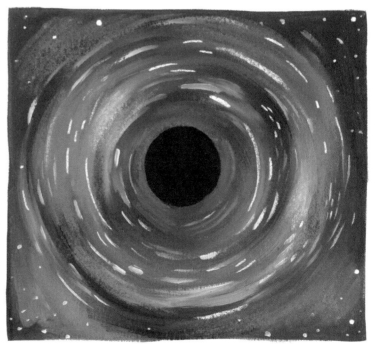

The star now disappears from view. . . and the black hole returns to hide in the shadows of space once more.

A Bolt of Lightning
Turns Sand to Glass

A strike of lightning on a hot summer's day at the beach can create one of nature's most fascinating works of art.

A large, towering thundercloud breaks the summer sunshine, and a flash of lightning strikes.

If the lightning strikes a sandy beach, the immense heat of the lightning bolt can melt grains of sand together. The produces delicate tubes of glass called 'fulgurites'. Let's watch one form before our eyes. . .

There's a flash of lightning on the horizon, then a long, low rumble of thunder. Clap!

The air around a bolt of lightning can reach 30,000 degrees Celsius – five times the temperature of the surface of the Sun!

A jagged bolt of lightning splits the sky in two. Zap!

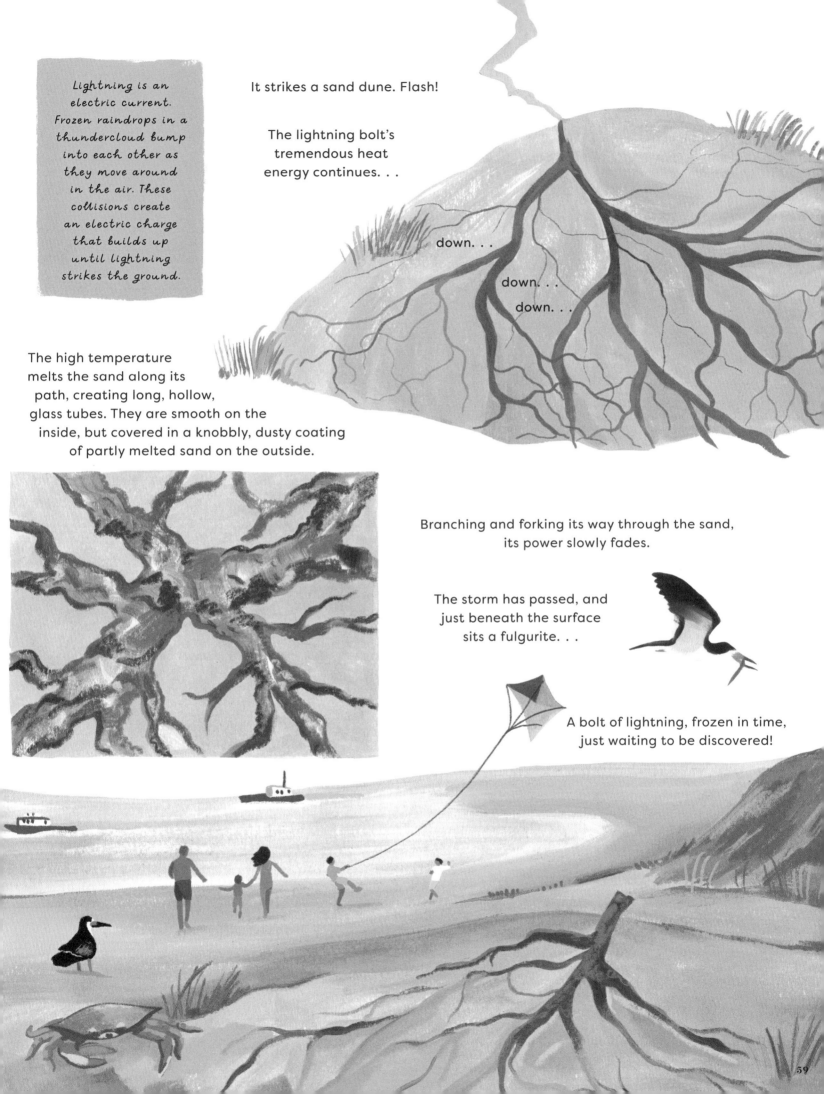

Lightning is an electric current. Frozen raindrops in a thundercloud bump into each other as they move around in the air. These collisions create an electric charge that builds up until lightning strikes the ground.

It strikes a sand dune. Flash!

The lightning bolt's tremendous heat energy continues. . .

down. . .

down. . .

down. . .

The high temperature melts the sand along its path, creating long, hollow, glass tubes. They are smooth on the inside, but covered in a knobbly, dusty coating of partly melted sand on the outside.

Branching and forking its way through the sand, its power slowly fades.

The storm has passed, and just beneath the surface sits a fulgurite. . .

A bolt of lightning, frozen in time, just waiting to be discovered!

A Cat's Eyes
Glow in the Dark

Two bright lights glare out of the darkness...

Like many night-time hunters, cats have a special reflective layer at the back of their eyes to help them to see in the dark.

If you catch a startled cat in the beam of a torch, you'll see a pair of glinting dots staring back at you... But what makes them glow?

It's a dark evening and Cat is on the prowl.
She saunters past a motion sensor and light illuminates a patch of the garden.

The light sweeps across the outline of the plant pots and hits the eyes of Cat. . . looking at her prey!

The light enters Cat's pupils – the small black holes in the centre of her eye's irises.

Below the surface of her eyes, the light travels on through the lens, which focuses it on to the retinas at the back of her eyeballs and creates a glow known as 'eyeshine'.

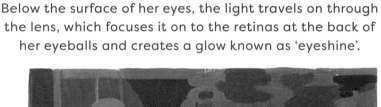

The light then hits a special iridescent layer just beneath the retinas, before bouncing straight back through it – increasing Cat's ability to see in low light – and back out of her eyes the same way it came in. . .

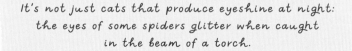

It's not just cats that produce eyeshine at night: the eyes of some spiders glitter when caught in the beam of a torch.

But as quickly as it appeared, it's gone again. Cat's eyeshine disappears as she turns away from the light to pounce on her prey!

The Salty Sea
Keeps a Swimmer Afloat

Lie back and gently float in the ocean, your toes wiggling above the water.

If you've ever been in the ocean, you may have noticed that it's much easier to float in than a swimming pool.

The difference between the water in the ocean and the water in a swimming pool – or even your bathtub – is salt! The more salt there is, the easier you'll bob about. But how do you stay afloat rather than sink like a stone? Let's dive in to find out. . .

This swimmer splashes into the turquoise ocean, his arms and legs propelling his body through the warm water.

He begins to feel tired, so he rolls on to his back, tilts his chin up and stretches out his arms and legs into a star shape.

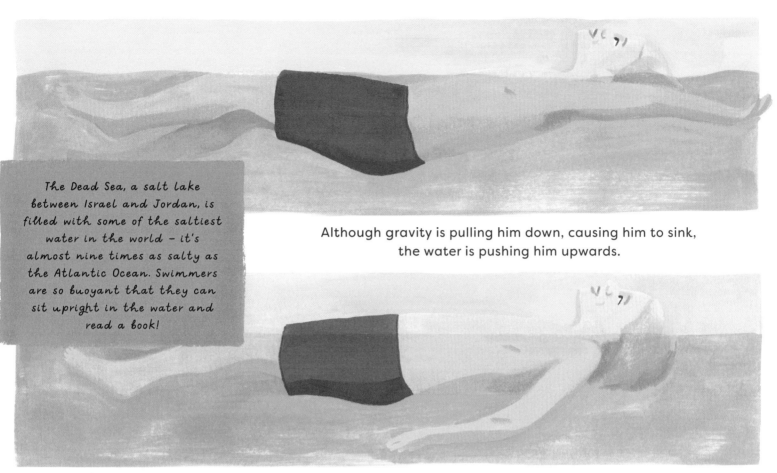

The Dead Sea, a salt lake between Israel and Jordan, is filled with some of the saltiest water in the world – it's almost nine times as salty as the Atlantic Ocean. Swimmers are so buoyant that they can sit upright in the water and read a book!

Although gravity is pulling him down, causing him to sink, the water is pushing him upwards.

His body weighs less than the water he is displacing and so he floats! This is called 'buoyancy'.

Lying on his back, he doesn't move a muscle. . . peacefully staring at the birds in the bright blue sky above.

Now he's had a rest, he can begin his journey back to shore. . . where an ice cream is waiting for him!

Water Freezes to Ice
on a Pond

Brrr... it's a cold evening in the garden as ice begins to form on the pond's surface.

Ice is the common name for frozen water.

Water can exist in three forms: as a solid (ice), a liquid (water) or a gas (steam). It all depends on how hot – or cold! – it is. So let's wrap up warm and wait patiently for this pond to freeze...

The Moon is big and bright as night falls at the end of a crisp winter's day.

In the pond, tiny liquid particles formed of hydrogen and oxygen bump into each other.

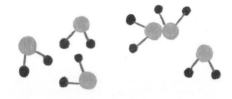

As the water gets colder, the tiny particles slow down... and then stop moving.

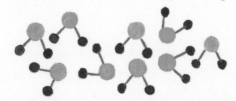

The particles join together in a lattice pattern to form a solid layer – ice!

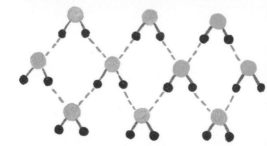

A thin sheet of ice slowly spreads across the pond's surface.

As the temperature continues to drop, the sheet of ice gets thicker and thicker. . .

Unlike almost all other liquids, water expands as it freezes. This means ice floats on water - and will burst pipes in cold weather!

And when morning comes, there is a glistening layer of ice across the entire pond.

But as the sun rises, spreading heat across the garden, the ice melts. . . until another cold night falls and the cycle begins again.

Quicksand Swallows
a Wellington Boot

Squelch! Squerch! A patch of sand has turned into a hungry monster!

When sand becomes saturated with water it can turn into a liquid goo called quicksand.

The surface seems solid, but as soon as you stand on it, the sand begins to shift and ooze, creeping around your feet and sucking at your wellies. Quicksand can be very dangerous, and before you know it, you're getting a sinking feeling. . .

Quicksand can develop anywhere, but is most likely on beaches, in marshes and near rivers. It can be caused by earthquakes suddenly shaking the ground, bringing water to the surface and turning the soil into a soupy liquid.

While this beachgoer combs the sand for shells, the tide goes out and reveals a boggy area called quicksand.

The sand is saturated with seawater and, beneath the surface, a spring carries more water upwards.

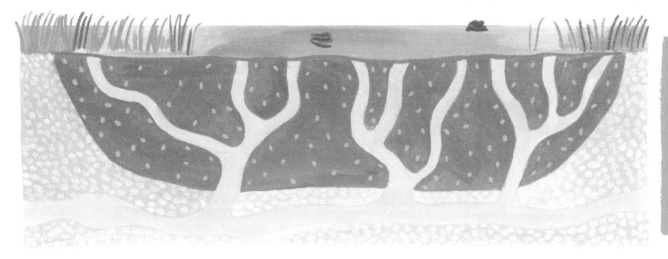

The rising seawater forces the grains of sand apart, reducing the friction between them and making the surface unstable.

As the boy steps on to the quicksand, his weight and the vibration of his steps jiggle the sand grains apart. . .

And his foot begins to sink down. . . down. . . down. . .

By moving slowly and spreading his weight evenly, he pulls his foot free. Pop!

But leaves his wellington boot behind. Oops!

A Glacier Retreats
Up an Alpine Valley

Like a slow-moving river, a large mass of ice scours out a valley as it flows...

High in the mountains in sheltered spots, snowfall can build up over many years and slowly turn to solid ice to become a 'glacier'.

As more snow falls, the ice becomes thicker and heavier, and the glacier's weight slowly draws it down the mountain. But as temperatures rise and the snow and ice melts, the glacier stops growing and begins to retreat uphill...

High in the mountainous Alps, snow falls on the glacier in the cold winter months.

As spring arrives, the snow begins to fade, and beautiful wildflowers carpet the alpine hillsides.

With the arrival of summer, warm air causes the surface of the glacier to melt and evaporate. . .

Meanwhile, the glacier's end, or 'snout', is melting fast, pouring away in a vast torrent of meltwater that flows down the mountain and eventually into the sea.

As months pass, and summer turns to autumn, the glacier diminishes dramatically – there is less new ice forming high up the mountain to feed it and the snout of the glacier retreats up the valley, moving higher and higher. . .

and the glacier begins to shrink.

The majority of the world's glaciers have been retreating for at least 30 years because of global warming.

Eventually, the glacier disappears completely – leaving just a jumble of rocks behind where a vast river of ice once flowed.

A Total Solar Eclipse
Brings Darkness During the Day

Once every year or two, a strange occurrence can be seen in the sky.

The Moon's path – which isn't always exactly the same – causes it to pass directly between the Sun and the Earth.

As the Moon covers the Sun, it blocks out the light causing a total solar eclipse. Let's put on our special eclipse glasses and look up as a dark shadow falls across the land, turning day to night.

It's a clear summer's day, the Sun is shining and there isn't a cloud in the sky.

Gradually, little by little, the light dims as the Moon begins to pass between the Earth and the Sun.

Although the Sun is 400 times larger than the Moon, it is also 400 times further away from the Earth. This means that the two objects appear the same size in the sky.

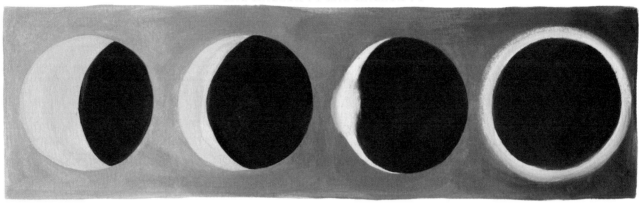

Until the Sun is entirely covered by the Moon, leaving only a fiery ring of sunlight called the 'corona'.

A total solar eclipse occurs every one or two years and is only visible from a small area on Earth each time.

Darkness falls. Birds stop singing and some flowers close.
This state is called 'totality' and can last as long as seven minutes.

Eventually, the Moon moves on. The Sun emerges, the sky begins to brighten and daylight returns once more.

A Current Carries
a Coconut Across the Sea

The restless ocean is always on the move...

Its tides ebb and flow, and there are strong currents that can carry everything, from seeds to ships.

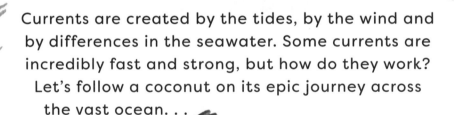

Currents are created by the tides, by the wind and by differences in the seawater. Some currents are incredibly fast and strong, but how do they work? Let's follow a coconut on its epic journey across the vast ocean...

This coconut tree is bending and swaying in the breeze, its palm fronds rustling.

As a coconut comes loose, it falls to the sand below. Thud!

The tides – the rise and fall of the sea – are caused by the gravitational pull of the Sun and the Moon.

The tide rises and the waves lift the coconut from the sandy floor.

As the tide falls, a current pulls the coconut towards the open water. Its journey begins. . .

Out at sea, the wind blows across the ocean's surface, creating a current that transports the coconut further out until the land slips below the horizon.

Differences in the temperature and salinity (the amount of salt) of parts of the sea cause currents that keep the oceans swirling about across vast distances and send the coconut on. . . and on. . .

Many seeds travel thousands of kilometres before germinating thanks to ocean currents, and animals can hitch a ride on a raft of floating vegetation too. Scientists think this was how lemurs moved from continental Africa to the island of Madagascar millions of years ago!

Until it washes ashore on the other side of the ocean, ready to be cracked open by this hungry monkey!

Coconuts can survive for months at sea because they are enclosed in a thick, fibrous, waterproof case that helps them float and protects the inner seed.

An Earthquake Rumbles

As a red panda naps in a tree, deep beneath the ground changes are afoot...

The Earth's crust, or outer layer, is made up of large pieces of rock called 'tectonic plates'.

These move very slowly, and the places where they meet are called 'faults'. As these plates move, they can rub against each other, releasing waves of energy. We feel this on the Earth's surface as an earthquake. Wait, what's that? Can you hear a rumble?

Deep underground, two tectonic plates are slowly moving, grinding against each other as they travel in different directions or at different speeds.

This rubbing causes friction, which makes the surfaces of the two tectonic plates stick together, and pressure builds up.

Under the immense pressure, the rock reaches breaking point. The two tectonic plates give way, slipping past each other and releasing the energy through the ground.

The energy travels outwards in a series of vibrations called seismic waves, rippling through the rock in all directions, rumbling across the forest floor.

The point where the rock breaks is known as the 'focus' of the earthquake, and the point directly above that on the earth's surface is called the 'epicentre' of the earthquake.

Snow falls from leaves; branches move from side to side and Red Panda wakes from his nap! The ground begins to shake. . .

Crash! Red Panda watches as trees fall to the ground.

After several moments, the earthquake stops. Phew! Red Panda waits until it's safe to wander the forest again.

A Stone Skips
Across a Lake

When the warm sun shines down on a calm lake, it's the perfect time to skim stones.

A flat, round stone, thrown with just the right spin, will seem to defy gravity, skipping across the surface of the water.

Let's watch a stone as it skips across a lake. . . How many times will it bounce?

With a flick of the wrist, the stone flies low and goes down. . .

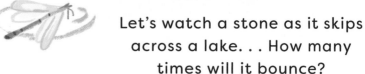

down. . .

down. . .

down. . .

towards the still surface of the lake, spinning to stay stable in flight.

As the stone hits the surface, it pushes the water up in front of itself, creating a slight wave. . .

which the stone races up like a ramp. . .

before taking flight again!

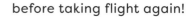

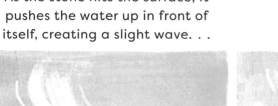

With each bounce the stone hops on. . . and on. . . and on. . .

The current stone-skimming world record is a colossal 88 skips!

Until finally the stone slows down, breaking the water's surface.

After nine whopping bounces, the stone sinks to the lakebed below.

A Glitter Path
Leads the Way

As the Sun sets over the ocean, a streak of golden light stretches towards the horizon. . .

During the day, the Sun beats down on the surface of the sea, its rays scattered in all directions by the waves. As the Sun sinks in the sky, the light forms a glittering ribbon across the surface of the water.

Seafarers can use these light patterns to show where hidden sandbanks and strong currents lie, which helps them to navigate shallow coastal waters.

After a long day at sea, this fisherman is ready to return home. But which way is home?

As the Sun sinks lower in the sky, it turns the horizon a fiery orange. . .

The Sun's rays are reflected by thousands of tiny ripples on the surface of the ocean.

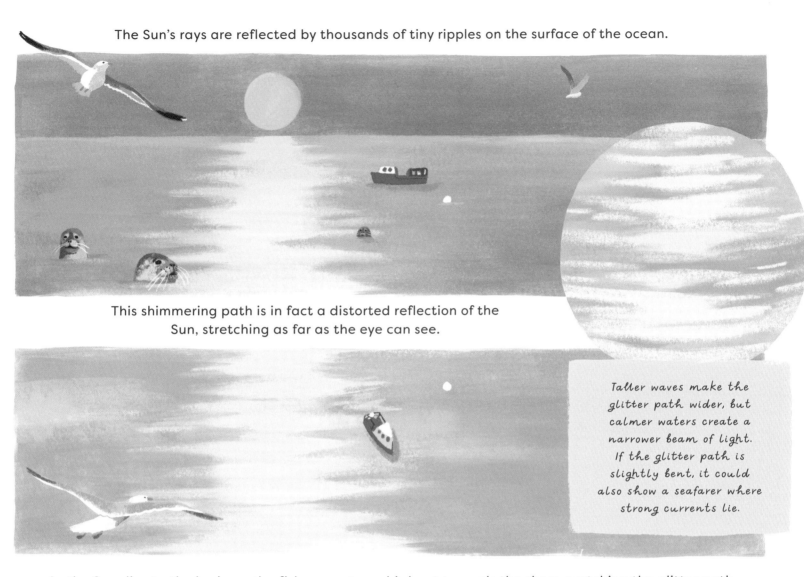

This shimmering path is in fact a distorted reflection of the Sun, stretching as far as the eye can see.

Taller waves make the glitter path wider, but calmer waters create a narrower beam of light. If the glitter path is slightly bent, it could also show a seafarer where strong currents lie.

As the Sun dips to the horizon, the fisherman turns his boat towards the shore, watching the glitter path for hints of hidden sandbars that cause ripples and small waves on the surface of the water. . .

until they are safely home.

The Universe
Explodes into Life

Around 13.8 billion years ago, the universe burst into existence with an almighty bang. . .

Today, the vast universe stretches in all directions and is filled with millions upon millions of stars, galaxies and unknown planets.

But how did it all begin?

In the beginning, there was nothing but a tiny, infinitely dense point, containing all the matter in the universe. When all of a sudden, this point exploded in a Big Bang, expanding and stretching in all directions, on and on. . .

The universe was filled with a dense, glowing plasma fog until almost 400,000 years after the Big Bang.

When the plasma fog cleared, there was a flash of light that scientists can still detect today.

But as there were no stars yet, darkness returned.

The universe continued to expand and cool, and atoms formed before coming together in gas clouds. . .

400 million years after the Big Bang, the gas clouds collapsed to create the first stars and galaxies.

The universe was 9 billion years old when our solar system appeared, the Sun igniting and the planets slowly forming from leftover dust and gas.

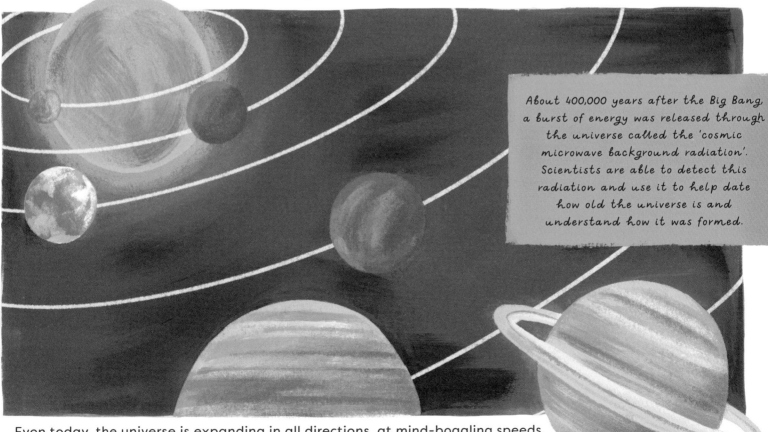

About 400,000 years after the Big Bang, a burst of energy was released through the universe called the 'cosmic microwave background radiation'. Scientists are able to detect this radiation and use it to help date how old the universe is and understand how it was formed.

Even today, the universe is expanding in all directions, at mind-boggling speeds, driven by a mysterious force called 'dark energy' that scientists are only just beginning to understand. . .

Connect with Nature

Now that you've witnessed natural wonders unfold, it's time to experience them for yourself. This evening, take some time to go outside and connect with the great outdoors... and then watch how it changes the way you see and hear the nature around you.

Come to a comfortable position lying on your back.

Let your hands rest on your tummy, fingertips lightly touching in front of your belly button.

Begin to breathe deeply, through your nose and mouth, down your throat, into your chest.

Open your eyes.
What can you see?

A night owl. . .

A full moon. . .

A twinkling star
in the night sky.

Open your ears.
What can you hear?

A hungry fox. . .

A little mouse. . .

The trees gently swishing,
all around you.

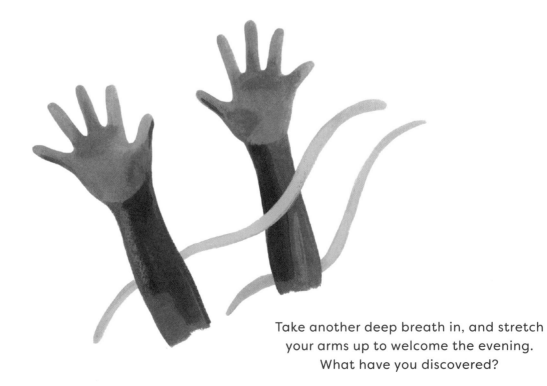

Take another deep breath in, and stretch
your arms up to welcome the evening.
What have you discovered?

Index

Further Reading

Find out more about the natural wonders of the world with the help of an adult.

Explorify
explorify.wellcome.ac.uk

Brilliant free resource from the Wellcome Trust, packed with information and activities to inspire curiosity about the natural world.

HowStuffWorks
howstuffworks.com

This site answers all the big questions that you may have about how the world works – and many small ones you've probably never realized you wanted answering too!

NASA
nasa.gov

The US space agency website has lots of inspiring information about satellites, stargazing, space exploration and much more.

National Geographic for Kids
natgeokids.com

A magazine and online portal stuffed with fun facts about our world, information about animals, science, history and geography, plus activities to do at home.

National Trust
nationaltrust.org.uk

Europe's largest conservation charity, the trust cares for and protects everything from coastlines to countryside, historic buildings and ancient woodlands.

Natural History Museum
nhm.ac.uk

Explore the museum's 80 million specimens, which span billions of years, or learn about natural history at home with lots of online activities.

Royal Botanic Gardens, Kew
kew.org

Learn about the power and beauty of plants and fungi in the stunning botanic gardens – and access home learning resources online.

Science Museum
sciencemuseum.org.uk

Britain's leading science museum with a huge collection of displays covering science, technology, engineering, mathematics and medicine – 250,000 of which can be viewed online.

The Smithsonian Institution
si.edu

A collection of nineteen museums and a zoo in the USA, the institution offers access to fascinating objects shedding light on science and nature.

ThoughtCo.
thoughtco.com

Comprehensive online guides to everything from animals to nature, written by experts.

Whale Trust
whaletrust.org

An organization based in Hawaii, USA researching the natural behaviour of whales in the Pacific Ocean and around the world.

The Wildlife Trusts
wildlifetrusts.org

These trusts provide a voice for a collection of 46 individual wildlife charities that support and protect wildlife and wild places across Britain.

Woodland Trust
woodlandtrust.org.uk

A charitable trust dedicated to planting, protecting and restoring woodland across Britain, with lots of information online about trees, plants and woodland creatures.

Selected Bibliography

BBC Bitesize, 'Earthquakes':
bbc.co.uk/bitesize/guides/ztp2k7h/revision/1

BBC Bitesize, 'Photosynthesis':
bbc.co.uk/bitesize/guides/zpwmxnb/revision/1

BBC Science Focus, 'Why do earthworms surface after rain?':
sciencefocus.com/nature/why-do-earthworms-surface-after-rain

Event Horizon Telescope, 'First-ever Image of a Black Hole Captured':
eventhorizontelescope.org

First Nature, 'Fairy ring champignon mushroom':
first-nature.com/fungi/marasmius-oreades

How Stuff Works, 'How quicksand works':
science.howstuffworks.com/environmental/earth/geology/quicksand

NASA, 'How do we launch things into space?':
spaceplace.nasa.gov/launching-into-space

NASA, 'Solar System Exploration':
solarsystem.nasa.gov/planets/overview

NASA, 'What is gravity?':
spaceplace.nasa.gov/what-is-gravity

National Geographic, 'Solar eclipses explained':
nationalgeographic.com/science/space/solar-system/solar-eclipse-article

National Ocean Service, 'Ocean currents':
oceanservice.noaa.gov/podcast/apr14/mw123-currents

National Trust, 'The Needles Headland and Tennyson Down':
nationaltrust.org.uk/the-needles-headland-and-tennyson-down

Natural History Museum, 'How are dinosaur fossils formed?':
nhm.ac.uk/discover/how-are-fossils-formed

NOAA, Earth System Research Laboratory, 'Glittering light on water':
psl.noaa.gov/outreach/education/science/glitter

NPR, 'Why do animals' eyes glow in the dark?':
npr.org/templates/story/story.php?storyId=96414364

Space, 'Our expanding universe':
space.com/52-the-expanding-universe-from-the-big-bang-to-today

Whale Trust, 'Whale song':
whaletrust.org/whale-song

Woodland Trust, 'What is a fairy ring and what causes them?':
woodlandtrust.org.uk/blog/2019/08/what-is-a-fairy-ring